The World's Most Popular Animals

Billy Grinslott & Kinsey Marie Books

ISBN - 9781965098240

I0115126

Dogs are the number one most popular animal in the world. The reason for that is many people have them for pets. So, it only makes sense that they are the most popular. The top 10 most popular dogs are. 1. French Bulldog, 2. Labrador Retriever. 3. Golden Retriever. 4. German Shepherd. 5. Poodle. 6. Bulldog. 7. Rottweiler. 8. Beagle. 9. Das hound. 10. German Shorthaired Pointer. No matter which dog you pick as a pet, they make great pals and partners.

Cats are the number 2 most popular animal in the world. Many people have cats as pets. Cats can be less demanding and are easier to care for. The top 10 most popular dogs are. 1. Ragdoll, 2. Main coon cat, 3. Devon Rex, 4. Exotic shorthair, 5. Persian, 6. British shorthair, 7. Abyssinian, 8 Non-Pedigreed Cats, 9 Scottish Fold, 10 Sphynx. No matter which cat you pick, they make great house pets. They like to play, cuddle and love attention.

Guinea pigs were one of the first domesticated smaller animals. Guinea pigs are highly intelligent and can communicate using a variety of sounds. They are not actually related to pigs. Guinea pigs make squealing and wheeking sounds like pigs, which may have contributed to the name. But the name guinea pig can also be traced back to their original price in England, where they could be bought for one guinea each. Either way they make good pets.

There are many types of rabbits in the wild. The most common is the cottontail. Rabbits are cute, friendly, and fun to watch. Many people have rabbits for pets. They have soft fluffy fur. They are called cottontails because they have a white fluffy tail that looks like a cotton ball.

Opossums or possums have strong tails and can hang from trees. One trick that a possum has, is when it feels danger is it will play dead. It will lay there and not move. Possums have white to gray face hair. Possums like to eat wood ticks. They are also immune to snakebites.

Hey what is that with the mask around its eyes. That is a raccoon. Raccoons like to come out at night. Their eyes are made so they can see in the dark. They are called masked bandits because they like to raid and eat out of trash cans at night.

Ringtails look like a racoon. They have stripes on their tails, but their face more resembles a cat. They are a member of the racoon family. Ringtails can be found in the south and southwestern parts of America. Ringtails are excellent climbers capable of ascending vertical walls, trees, rocky cliffs and even cactus. They are mostly nocturnal.

Meerkats are immune to some snakes venom as they belong to the mongoose family. Meercats can also eat scorpions because they are immune to their venom. Meerkats are smart and have problem solving capabilities. They can spot birds miles away. They have dark patches around their eyes to cut down glare from the sun and help them see far into the distance.

People love to have pet birds and enjoy bird watching. Some of the most widespread bird species include the House Sparrow, Common Starling, Rock Pigeon, and the Mallard duck. Some of the most common pet birds are Parakeets, Cockatiels, Finches and Parrots. Some of these house birds are fun, because you can teach them to say words.

Cockatoos are part of the parrot family. Cockatoos can mimic the sounds of other animals, including people. Cockatoos love to hold their food in their feet while eating. Cockatoos differ from other parrots, because they can raise their crest feathers up when needed, unlike other parrots.

Chickens are the most raised bird on a farm. Male chickens, Roosters wake up every morning and make a loud crowing noise that can be heard for miles. Hens, female chickens lay eggs daily and they are collected and sold to stores for us to eat. Chickens have great memories & can recognize over 100 faces. Chickens can see in color. They dream when they sleep. Chickens have been around since the dinosaur days.

Sheep have a wool fur coat. Farmers will shave sheep and collect the wool to make clothing. Many clothes are made from the wool collected from sheep's fur. Their wool fur coat regrows forever so they can be shaven multiple times. Sheep are smart and can recognize up to 50 other sheep faces and remember them for two years. A baby sheep is called a lamb. If a sheep falls on it's back, it can't turn over to stand up again. They have nearly 360-degree vision and can see everything around them.

There are several types of goats on a farm, but the Billy goat has a memorable name. Goats were one of the first animals to be tamed by humans. Goats don't have teeth on their upper jaw. Goats have rectangular pupils. They have 4 stomachs. Goats have incredible agility and balance. Cashmere coats come from goats. Goats milk is the most popular milk worldwide.

Pigs are raised all over the world, and provide valuable products to humans, including pork, lard, leather, glue, fertilizer, and medicines. Pigs like to lay in mud because they can't sweat like humans, so they lay in the mud to cool off. Pigs are clean animals, and they are smarter than dogs. Mother pigs sing to their babies. Pigs dream and like to sleep nose-to-nose. They are very social and love it when you rub their belly.

Cows can be male or female. Male cows are usually called bulls and have horns. Females are called cows. Baby cows are called calf's. Female cows provide us with milk. Dairy farms raise many female cows for their milk. Milk is drank by many people and has lots of nutrients and vitamins. Cows have a visual field of 330° almost an all-around view. Cows don't need much sleep and can take a nap while standing up. Cows originated in Turkey. They are very social and like hanging out in groups.

Not only do people enjoy riding horses, but they are used for pulling things and for rounding up livestock. Horses were one of the first animals people used for riding on. Horses can't breathe through their mouth. Horses can sleep standing up. Horses have a nearly 360-degree field of vision. Horses do not have teeth in the middle of their mouth. Horses are highly intelligent animals. There are over 600 types of horses. They are good pets.

The whitetail deer is the most popular deer in North America. Whitetail deer have good eyesight and hearing. Only male deer grow antlers, which are shed each year. Whitetail deer are good swimmers and will use large streams and lakes to escape predators. A young deer is called a fawn. They are the most common deer species and live everywhere in North America.

Wolves, coyotes, and foxes are all part of the dog family. The timber wolf, also known as the gray wolf, is the largest wolf in North America. Wolves are legendary because of their spine-tingling howl, which they use to communicate. Their territory size is 25 to 150 square miles. They like to roam in packs of 2 to 25 wolves. You can see gray and red wolves in many areas.

Most popular world bear species are · Black Bear · Brown Bear · Polar Bear · Asiatic black bear · Andean Bear · Panda Bear · Sun bear. There are many different species of black bears in the world. Black bears are one of the smallest members of the bear family. The black bear is the most common, of the bear species found in the world. Not all black bears are completely black, some have different fur colors and features.

Panda bears are one of the most famous. Giant pandas live in a few mountain ranges in south central China, in Sichuan, Shaanxi and Gansu provinces. Like domestic cats, giant panda bears have vertical slits for pupils on their eyes. Giant pandas are good swimmers and excellent tree climbers. Giant pandas spend 10-16 hours a day feeding, mainly on bamboo.

Grizzly bears are one of the most feared bears in the world. They are well known for being in movies. Grizzly bears are a subspecies of the brown bear. They are called Grizzly bears because they have silver tips on their hair, a grizzled look. The hump on a Grizzly bear's back is a huge muscle. Grizzly bears don't hibernate like other bears. They are highly intelligent, have excellent memories and great smell. They are good swimmers and fast runners.

The Polar Bear is one of the biggest bears on earth. Male polar bears can weigh up to 1500 lbs. Female polar bears weigh about half as much as males. They like swimming and can swim constantly for days at a time. Polar bears keep warm thanks to the blubber under their skin. They can smell up to a mile away. Polar bears spend most of their time at sea. They can run 25 mph, and they can swim up to 10mph. There's still a debate of whether the Kodiak bear or the polar bear is the biggest bear in the world.

There are many monkeys and chimpanzees in the world. The most popular is the spider monkey. Spider monkeys have strong tails and can hang from them. They Don't Have Thumbs like other monkeys. They are swinging specialists. They are social animals and like to hang out in groups.

Gorillas have hands and feet like humans including thumbs and big toes. Some gorillas in captivity have learned to use sign language to communicate with humans. Gorillas pound their chest as a type of communication. People share around 98% of our DNA with gorillas. They are one of the biggest, most powerful living primates. They have 16 different types of calls. Gorillas live in small groups called troops or bands.

Many people have turtles as pets. The Red-Eared Slider Turtle is the most popular type of pet turtle on earth as well as the most common. Sliders spend lots of time basking in the sun. As cold-blooded animals, they need the sun to heat up. Red-eared slider turtles make active pets that enjoy swimming and diving. Red-eared slider turtles are very common, they live all around the world.

The most common seal is the crab-eater seal, whose numbers are estimated to be between 15 and 40 million. Crabeater seals do not actually eat crabs. Crabeater Seals have a unique adaptation for feeding. They have evolved a sieve-like tooth structure that filter krill. They suck in water containing krill, close their jaws, and then force the water back out between their specialized teeth, trapping the krill inside.

The bottlenose dolphin is the most popular. Bottlenose dolphins are found in temperate and tropical waters around the world. Bottlenose dolphins grow up to 13 feet long and 1,300 pounds. There are both short and long Bottlenose dolphins. They get their name from their snout that is shaped like a bottle.

The most common whale in the world is the dwarf or pygmy sperm whale, which is found in temperate and tropical waters worldwide The dwarf sperm whale is a small whale, about 8 feet in length and around 600 pounds. Dwarf sperm whales are very similar to the pygmy sperm whale. The dwarf sperm whale inhabits temperate and tropical oceans worldwide, in particular continental shelves and slopes.

Orcas, known as killer whales, are the largest member of the dolphin family. A male orca can be 32 feet in length and weigh 22 thousand pounds, as big as a school bus. Orcas are intelligent and able to coordinate maneuvers. Orcas are extremely fast swimmers. Orcas live in every ocean in the world. They sleep with one eye open and can see any other fish coming their way.

The Great White is the most feared shark in the world. They grow up to 20 feet long and weigh up to 6,600 pounds. Great White sharks existed before dinosaurs. A Great White can eat a whole seal and won't need to eat for another three months. They have 300 teeth in their mouth, that's a lot of teeth. Great whites are the largest predatory fish on earth. This awesome shark is found across the Pacific, Atlantic, and Indian Oceans.

Hippopotamus are also called a hippo. They are the second largest land animal. They have the largest mouth of any land animal. To stay cool, they spend most of their time in the water. Hippos can hold their breath for up to five minutes underwater. When submerged, their ears and nostrils fold shut to keep water out. They sweat an oily red liquid which helps protect their skin and acts as a sunblock, too! Cool, huh?

Rhinoceros are also called a rhino. They are huge and can run as fast as a car, up to 55 miles per hour. They have a long horn on their nose that is made from the same stuff as our fingernails. Rhinos have very poor eyesight. They communicate through honks and sneezes. They snort to warn other animals when they get to close. They love playing in the mud and water to keep cool and keep insects from biting them.

Male lions are known as the king of the jungle because of their raw power and strength. Lions don't fear other animals. The roar of a male lion can be heard 5 miles away. Lions like to live in groups known as a pride. Male lions have mains and females do not. Female lions gather most of the food and male lions protect the herd and the young cubs, baby lions.

Tigers are considered one of the most beautiful cats by many, because of their astonishing looks and black stripes. Tigers are the largest amongst all the wild cats. They are strong and can knock things down with one swipe of their paw. Tiger cubs are born blind until their eyes develop. Tigers live for 25 years, and they love to swim and play in the water.

Giraffes are the tallest mammal on earth. Their long legs and neck help them to eat leaves from the trees. They like to eat leaves. New-born baby giraffes are taller than most humans and they can stand within 30 minutes. Giraffes live up to 25 years. Giraffes can sleep standing up like a horse. Giraffes are super peaceful animals. They are easy to get along with.

Elephants are the largest land animal. They have huge ears. They can grab stuff with their trunks. Elephants eat all day long. They can't jump like other animals and humans. Elephants communicate with vibrations in the ground. Baby elephants can stand within 20 minutes after birth. Elephants are very smart. They never forget anything. Elephants purr like cats do.

Adelie's are the most widely distributed penguin species in the world. Adelie's penguins build their nests with stones and are known to steal stones from other penguin nests. They are known to rock back on their heel and prop themselves up on land utilizing their tail feathers. Adelie Penguins are very faithful to their family and nest sites. When Adelie penguin chicks are about nine weeks old, their downy baby feathers have been replaced by waterproof adult feathers. They live in some of the coldest places on earth.

King penguins are the most famous. King penguins don't build nests to lay eggs. They stand upright and incubate the egg on the tops of their feet under a loose fold of skin. The chicks hatch with no feathers and are dependent upon their parents until they grow them. King penguins have colorful feathers around their necks and heads, this makes them the brightest of all the species of penguin.

Author Page

Billy Grinslott & Kinsey Marie Books

ISBN – 9781965098240

Thanks

www.ingramcontent.com/pod-product-compliance
Lightning Source LLC
Chambersburg PA
CBHW060833270326
41933CB00002B/73